To: Va
So happy to meet you,
Enjoy!

When Douglas Met Dyrene

Journey of Friendship, Love,
Faith, and Commitment

Dyrene Penn Saulsberry

[signature]

1-1-25

CONTENTS

DEDICATION:

To Douglas: my husband, my soul mate, my best and forever friend, my rock, my partner for life, and the one who knows and understands me. Thank you for seeing my heart many years ago. Thank you for supporting me over the years with ALL my numerous projects!

Prologue

As you read this story, keep in mind the movie, *The Adjustment Bureau*. The characters in the movie were meant to be together but kept going on and off their course, seemingly never to connect. Unbeknownst to them, someone or *something* was always secretly working on their behalf. This invisible entity was constantly rerouting their decisions and paths to ensure that they would eventually meet, become best friends, fall in love, marry, and live a long and happy life together.

She would never forget that cold winter night in January when her whole world came crumbling down right in front of her face. She was hurt, distraught, and devastated! She asked the questions, "What have I done?","Why is this happening to me?","How could he be so cruel after all we had been through together?" She did not understand how he could hurt her. She felt abandoned by God and by the man she loved.

When Douglas Met Dyrene

CHAPTER 1:

DYRENE'S STORY

D yrene was the last child born to the late Joe and Izora Penn in the city of Shawmut, a small rural town in Alabama. She was the baby girl in a family of 13 children, and the family moved to Atlanta when Dyrene was still a toddler. She received her early education in the Atlanta Public School System, where she caught the "teaching bug." She admired her teachers' smarts and the sharp clothes they wore. Therefore, she decided she wanted to be a teacher as well. As a young girl, you could often find her playing school with her younger brother, Frankie, her childhood friend, Henrietta, and other children in the neighborhood. Every time they got together, Dyrene was *always* the teacher.

Upon graduating from L.J. Price High School, Dyrene attended Morris Brown College, an incredible HBCU in the Southeast. She knew she wanted to be a teacher, but she just could not make the adjustment at Morris Brown for some unexplained reason. Dyrene spent more time in the student union building playing bid whist than attending classes. When you get her in a bid whist game today, she often boasts that she majored in the popular card game. In addition, she was also still hanging out with her high school classmates who were not in school and who did not display dreams or aspirations of their own. The peer pressure she endured is precisely why Dyrene is a strong advocate of young people going *away* to college. Going away allows you to meet new people and not hang with the same crowd.

Dyrene's siblings were all gainfully employed in various fields. Two sisters were entrepreneurs who owned beauty salons. Three brothers served in the military, one of which was the U.S. Air Force's first African American Fire Inspector. Despite the successes of her older siblings, Dyrene still did not have a role model to help her navigate college life and keep her eyes on the prize. Even though she was the first in her family to attend college, she did not take college seriously.

Raised up in a Christian home, Dyrene understood the plans God had for her life from an early age. Jeremiah 29:11 states,

> "For I know the plans I have for you, declares the Lord, plans to prosper you and not to harm you, plans to give you hope for the future."

She realized the direction that she was headed while attending Morris Brown was *not* the path God had for her. Subsequently, after a year at Morris Brown, she packed her bags, bid her family farewell, and on October 20, 1970, she traveled to the Motor City where her father and older sister resided. This was by far the best decision she had ever made!

After relocating to Detroit, Dyrene immediately went to work at Michigan Bell Telephone Company. While working there, she met Deborah, her best friend of over 50 years. The two worked as office assistants for 15 all-white male artists in the Yellow Pages Art Department on Oakman Boulevard. Deborah was already attending Wayne County Community College (WCCC), so she encouraged Dyrene to enroll. Despite all that had happened at Morris Brown, Dyrene had not given up on her dream of becoming a teacher. So, she got back on track, transferred what little credits she had accumulated at her previous school, and continued pursuing her lifelong goal. She earned her Associate's Degree from WCCC and transferred those credits to Wayne State University, where she enrolled in the College of Education. From here, the love story slowly begins to unfold.

Chapter 2:

Douglas's Story

Douglas was the seventh and last child born to the late Rev. Thomas and Clara Saulsberry in Detroit, Michigan. He was born and raised on the southwest side of Detroit in a community of Black and Hispanic families, near the Ambassador Bridge that connects two countries: Canada and the United States of America.

Douglas attended Detroit Public Schools,

and I guess you can say it was expected for him to attend college. After all, four siblings were school teachers; one brother was a physician, and another brother a professional entertainer.

Douglas's goal was to be a secretary. He was motivated by one of his sisters who was taking business classes at Commerce High School. Also, the secretarial field was dominated by women; therefore, it was a perfect profession to meet females. As an adult, he is known as Mr. Cool and Mr. Smooth. He also had that "cool" and "smooth" thang going on back in high school. When Douglas entered Western International High School, his curriculum consisted of business classes. Following that business path, he also worked at Winkelman's women's clothing store through the Co-op student program.

Throughout high school, Douglas enjoyed singing in talent shows and performing at various events around the city. His singing group, The Politicians, received rave reviews everywhere they performed. Young ladies were mesmerized by Douglas's melodious tenor voice. During performances, he made many, young and old, scream, holler, and faint. He could have had his pick of women. Hands down, The Politicians were an up-and-coming group destined for fame and fortune. They were just as talented as groups like the Temptations and Four Tops, but The Adjustment Bureau was not having it. Why? Douglas had to stay on course and meet Dyrene.

Unfortunately, a member of the Politicians was killed. After that incident, Douglas left the group and his desire to be a professional entertainer behind.

After graduating from Western International High School, Douglas enrolled in Wayne County Community College (WCCC), where he, of course, took business classes. Douglas attended WCCC for a while and simultaneously worked part-time jobs, including Winkelman's, Red Run Golf Course, and Lear Siegler Steel Company. Unfortunately, he got hooked on the "Benjamins." As a result, he quit school and went to work full time at Michigan Tractor. Although Douglas was bringing in lots of dough, he was not satisfied.

With all that had happened, it appeared

Douglas was on the path to becoming a secretary or a world-famous singer/performer. Keep in mind that one of his brothers was a professional entertainer, *and* he was attracted to the world of business through one of his sisters. Unfortunately, the Adjustment Bureau would not allow Douglas to go in either direction. It had other plans for Douglas. Remember, he had four siblings who were educators. One could surmise that teaching was in his blood. Therefore, he was destined to attend college and become a teacher as well. Additionally, he was not aware, but he had to take the teaching route if he were to meet Dyrene.

One fall day, Douglas had an epiphany. He walked into Michigan Tractor, where he was making all that dough, and *quit* his job. He transferred his credits from Wayne County Community College to Wayne State University to enroll in the College of Education. Douglas had contemplated something his brother Oscar shared with him before graduating from high school. Oscar told him, "By the time you graduate from high school, all your siblings will be finished with college; we can pay for you to go to school." Douglas had the perfect role models and benefactors. How could he lose? Inquiring minds want to know: Did Douglas *really* get a free ride, compliments of his siblings? We may never truly know the answer, but we do know what happens next is one for the books.

Chapter 3:

A Friendship is Born

The chances of Douglas and Dyrene's meeting were slim to none. After all, they grew up and lived hundreds of miles apart. Even after Dyrene relocated to Michigan, they ran in different circles in Detroit. Living in their own two worlds, they pursued their long-life dreams and searched for "Mr. Right" and "Mrs. Right." Through their quest to find that special person, Dyrene and Douglas experienced failed relationships, heartaches, and pain along the way. Nevertheless, no matter what happened in their lives, all roads led them to each other—no doubt the Adjustment Bureau at work.

In 1976, Douglas and Dyrene were both taking classes in the College of Education at Wayne State University. Ironically, they were never scheduled a class together. Still, as fate would have it, they both eventually enrolled in one of Dr. Paula Wood's education classes. Interestingly enough, their class was held on different days, so they never crossed each other's paths.

One day, Dr. Wood posted a flyer on a bulletin board near her office, advertising volunteer opportunities in a Saturday water recreation program for children with autism. The program was held at the Detroit downtown branch YMCA. Douglas and Dyrene had good hearts, so it was no surprise that they both signed up for the volunteer program.

They showed up at the YMCA on the beautiful, crisp morning of Saturday, September 25, 1976. The sun was shining bright, and the leaves were beginning to display their vibrant colors. The program started at 10:00 a.m. In keeping with the Douglas thang that Dyrene has grown to know and love, Douglas arrived LATE. He introduced himself, and they exchanged pleasantries before receiving instructions from the volunteer coordinator. Dyrene did not see Douglas as a love interest when they met. After all, she was already in a relationship. Obviously, Douglas was not interested in Dyrene either. Nevertheless, a beautiful friendship was born.

Chapter 4:

The Seed: Platonic Friendship (1976-1985)

Douglas and Dyrene fulfilled their lifelong dreams. They both graduated from Wayne State University, earning their Bachelor of Science Degrees in Special Education. Later, they both received their Master of Education Degree and Education Specialist Certifications. Upon graduation, Douglas began teaching in Grosse Pointe Schools. He later secured a position with Detroit Public Schools Adult

Education Department. Dyrene accepted an assignment at Oakman Orthopedic School in Detroit Public Schools. As time went on, Douglas landed a position in the same school where Dyrene was assigned. Again, the Adjustment Bureau was at work. The transfer allowed their friendship to take root and blossom. They and their friend Patricia (Patty) were often seen sitting together in staff meetings, having lunch together, and regularly hanging out after work hours.

Douglas had a relationship with Christ, and he believed in sharing the Lord with his friends. Not only did Douglas and Dyrene have a good working relationship as friends, but their friendship was also nurtured and molded in the spiritual realm. On several occasions, he invited Dyrene and her friends to worship with him at Greater Southern Missionary Baptist Church, where his father, the late Rev. Thomas Saulsberry, was the founding pastor. In addition, Douglas sang in the choir and was an usher.

Even when Douglas went out on Saturday nights, he still made it to Sunday worship service. Eventually, Dyrene joined Greater Southern and served as an usher, Sunday School teacher, and a member of the Rev. Thomas and Clara Saulsberry Scholarship Staff.

***

As mentioned earlier, Dyrene was in a relationship when she and Douglas met. She got married after graduating from college, but her marriage ended in a divorce due to "irreconcilable differences."

Meanwhile, Dyrene did what any typical young lady would do. She got up, dusted herself off, and started dating again. She believed in the institution of marriage, so she married again and had a baby girl named Dorinda Denise, who God called home after being on this planet for a short while. That marriage could not withstand the storms and pressures of life either. Subsequently, Dyrene found herself divorced...again.

Douglas was an incredibly supportive friend to Dyrene, seeing her through two divorces and the death of her baby girl. He was always a friend, and they shared a special bond. When people experience trials and tribulations within their relationships, it is a blessing to know you have a friend you can count on. Douglas and Dyrene's friendship remained solid through the ups and downs. They truly cherished their unique friendship and were happy to be there for each other.

In the meantime, Douglas was doing what any average handsome, intelligent, and eligible bachelor did. He dated! Although he went on many dates, Douglas never got married. When asked why he said he could not find that "special one." However, Douglas did have a son, Jacob Kali, whom he loves very much!

No matter what relationship they were in, Douglas and Dyrene maintained their friendship. They always welcomed each other's love interest into their relationship. Their love interests even admired the friendship Douglas and Dyrene were blessed to know and experience. They racked up nine years as platonic friends. While the Adjustment Bureau celebrated the years Douglas and Dyrene had accumulated as friends, their assignment was not over. They had to create a situation that would cause Douglas and Dyrene to pay attention to each other. The inevitable had to happen.

Chapter 5:

To Be or Not to Be...
More than Friends

Dyrene and Douglas did not think of becoming more than friends. When Douglas's relationship with his son's mother ended, Dyrene tried to hook him up with a "good woman," their friend Patty, because Douglas was a "good man." Dyrene wanted nothing but the best for Douglas. Unfortunately, Patty did not take the bait, saying she was struggling to make an impossible relationship work and was not open to the idea. The Adjustment Bureau was not open to that idea either. After all, their assignment was to hook up Douglas and Dyrene, not Douglas and Patty.

Douglas and Dyrene had to become more than friends because the Adjustment Bureau's assignment was to bring them together as a couple. And… the Adjustment Bureau *always* completed its assignments. They had never botched up a mission, and they certainly were not going to fail *this* one.

Chapter 6:

The Kiss

By March 1985, circumstances rendered Douglas and Dyrene both free agents, so to speak. For the first time since meeting, they were no longer in committed relationships. Then, the most amazing and wonderful thing happened: Douglas kissed Dyrene! This incident occurred after the death of Douglas's father. Dyrene was shocked! She brushed it off, thinking Douglas was simply mourning the loss of his father. Therefore, he surely could not be thinking clearly.

After the kiss, they looked at each other through different lenses, which changed the dynamics of their relationship. Had they stepped across the line? They wondered whether their friendship would suffer because of "the kiss." Could the kiss ruin their longtime friendship they were so proud of and had developed over time? Only time would tell.

Dyrene was poised to introduce Douglas to yet another friend before the kiss. In that instant, she changed her mind. She had never felt that kind of passion before. Electricity vibrated through her entire body. The keys she was holding in her hand dropped to the floor. She trembled from the energy of the fire pouring through the innermost parts of her body. She thought to herself, *I'm keeping him for myself.*

Douglas and Dyrene decided to explore the possibility of being more than friends. After all, they already had a foundation and enjoyed each other's company very much. In addition, they were blessed with the opportunity very few couples get—to get a bird's eye view into each other's character, behavior, and interactions within different relationships. Douglas was a one-woman man, and Dyrene did not believe in straying while in a relationship either.

At last, the Adjustment Bureau was satisfied. Mission accomplished! Or… so they thought.

CHAPTER 7:

TO DATE OR NOT TO DATE

Douglas and Dyrene were so excited about their newfound relationship. After all, they had been in and out of several while searching for Mr. and Mrs. Right. Initially, they were met with naysayers. Inquiring minds asked questions such as, "Why switch from friendship to courtship?", "Why change since you guys are good friends?" ,"Why now, after all these years?" All questions to which Douglas and Dyrene did not have answers.

At first, a woman from Douglas's past even tried to sabotage their relationship, throwing darts and arrows every chance she got. However, Douglas and Dyrene did not let those who objected to their relationship deter them. They felt deep down inside that this was the right thing to do. They prayed about their decision and sought God's guidance. Douglas and Dyrene stayed focused on each other and continued to follow their hearts.

Although there were many naysayers, the new couple did have the blessings of many. Among the numerous family and friends cheering them on was a particular aunt and nephew. Aunt Ardeatha and Daniel were thrilled about Douglas and Dyrene's new relationship. In fact, their announcement as a couple was met with excitement and joy from all over. Finally, it seemed as if things were moving in a positive direction.

CHAPTER 8:

EXCLUSIVE DATING

(1985-1990)

Over time, their friendship evolved into a beautiful court-ship. They appreciated going out to concerts, the movies, long romantic walks in the park, fine dining, traveling, and attending church together. They even reveled in the friendly competition of planning spe-cial events and outings for each other's birthdays to outdo each other. For example, a special outing could have included a train ride to a secret location, a romantic cruise or limo ride to a special dinner with strolling violinists, plays on Broadway, etc.

They also looked forward to simple outings such as their weekly Saturday drive to Al's Seafood at the Eastern Market in Detroit. While there, they indulged in delicious fresh fried smelts and saltine crackers with hot sauce. These two fell in love, and they fell hard! While spending much of their time together, the couple grooved to the sounds of Frankie Beverly. Dyrene enjoyed being dined and wined, traveling around the world, and experiencing the finer things in life with the man she loved.

***

Douglas decided on the perfect Christmas gift for Dyrene for their first Christmas together. Douglas had a family member who lived in the Atlanta area who made beautiful sequin dresses and gowns. Each sequin is carefully sewn by hand, one stitch at a time. He had a dress made especially for her. The deadline for the post office to deliver packages by Christmas had passed. For the dress to reach Detroit by Christmas, the designer had to send it express via Greyhound.

It was a freezing morning with several inches of snow on the ground. Douglas left his home on the Westside of Detroit at 2:00 a.m. in frigid temperatures. He drove to downtown Detroit in heavy falling snow to pick up his package from the Greyhound Bus Terminal. He did not have a choice since it was Christmas morning, and he did not have an alternate gift for Dyrene. After all, Douglas was still wooing Dyrene and making good first impressions. Therefore, he had to get that package by any means necessary.

Douglas paced the floor back and forth in the terminal until the bus arrived. Later that morning, he walked out with Dyrene's gift in hand. He looked forward to presenting it to her that evening.

We do not know who was to blame, the designer or Douglas, for the delay in getting the package shipped for an on-time delivery via the Post Office. Truthfully, my money is on

Douglas since we now know he is notorious for procrastinating.

***

Every year, Dyrene planned a very special Christmas party for family and friends at her home. Everyone looked forward to her annual Christmas party, and she would never forget *this* particular year. It seemed *extra* special. Although each year they boast about picking the "perfect" tree, Douglas and Dyrene thought the tree that year topped all previous years. They decorated it together with African-inspired ornaments and were pleased with their final product.

Dyrene's Christmas decorations were spectacular that year. Her duplex was decorated from top to bottom. You knew it was

Christmas time from the moment you entered her place. The huge, beautifully decorated Christmas tree greeted you from a special corner of the living room. The staircase banister was adorned in wintergreen garland and large red bows that laced the staircase leading to the second level. You could find a little Christmas in every room.

Douglas and Dyrene spent the most beautiful Christmas holiday together that year, visiting with family and friends and attending holiday parties. Douglas seemed overly attentive that year, but Dyrene did not overthink it because her man was that kind of guy. They were a very happy couple, and it showed.

However, being just a couple was not

enough for Dyrene. Remember, she welcomed the institution of marriage. Dyrene never gave up on marriage. She *knew* with the right person, married life would be great. Dyrene did not believe she was meant to travel through life without being married to a loving, kind, and caring man. Hell, look at how many times she tried marriage! Still, She was not afraid to keep the faith and wait for Mr. Right.

In the meantime, Douglas was reluctant to make that commitment. He was 39, single, and never shacked up…let alone been married, for crying out loud. As Dyrene pushed, Douglas grew wearier and wearier. She did not realize that Douglas was getting ready to drop a bomb on her the following month.

Dyrene would never forget that cold winter night in January when her whole world came crumbling down right in front of her face. Douglas called off their courtship, stating that he could not give Dyrene what she wanted. She was hurt, distraught, and devastated! She asked the questions, "What have I done?", "Why is this happening to me?", "How could he be so cruel after all we have been through together?"

Ladies, in situations like this, isn't it strange how we always ask, "What have *I* done?" In many instances, *we* take the blame. Has it ever occurred to you that it is NOT "What have I done?" but rather, "What is he *not* doing?"

In this case, he did not want to take their relationship to the next level. She did not understand how he could hurt her. With no warning! He just disappeared! She felt abandoned by her God and by the man she loved. Dyrene's goal was to settle down into a long-lasting marriage. Douglas's goal was to stay single. They bid each other farewell. Ladies, no ultimatums!

Douglas and Dyrene enjoyed five years of exclusive dating until the day her world got turned upside down. She spent many nights crying herself to sleep. Like functioning drug addicts, she was a functioning, broken-hearted woman. Hell, LOVE is an addiction! She went to work every day, behaving as if everything was all right yet coming home and wallowing in her pain and misery. Through it all, Dyrene kept the faith. She prayed for God's will in her situation. She resorted to writing and displaying positive affirmations through-out her duplex to help keep her sanity. Dyrene also leaned on her longtime friend, Deborah, for sisterly and emotional support. Deborah had a large picture window in her living room with a huge window seat. They would sit on that window seat, and Deborah would comfort Dyrene by listening to whatever she had to say while they sipped on Southern Comfort Whiskey and hot tea. Dyrene thought she had lost the man of her dreams.

CHAPTER 9:

ADJUSTMENT BUREAU INTERVENES

The Adjustment Bureau had to come out of retirement to get Douglas and Dyrene back on course. They had never had such a complicated assignment in all of their years in the field. Nine years of platonic friendship had passed, exclusive dating, and now this!

Life for Douglas and Dyrene was miserable! These were awkward times for the two of them. It was difficult to avoid each other since they saw each other at staff meetings for the Special Education department and attended the same church. It was no getting around worshipping together. Instead of lingering around the church at the end of services and leaving together as they had done in previous years, one would leave before the other. They were always cordial in public, but they went out of their way to avoid each other. AWK-WARD!

After being separated for a while, they had the *audacity* to begin going out again to ease their heartache. They longed for and enjoyed each other's company very much! Subsequently, Douglas would invite Dyrene out to various events, and she would accept his invitations. However, he still was not trying to take that next step, although he knew her position.

After moping around for three months while seeing Douglas occasionally, Dyrene dusted herself off and tried dating again. That did not work. She looked for what she found in Douglas in other brothers she dated. Douglas was the total package: Christian, intelligent, sexy, and true. Unfortunately, *no one* lived up to Douglas's standards and qualities. The girl was absolutely *sprung*!

Meanwhile, it was never revealed how Douglas spent his time during their separation. However, one could guess that he was satisfied because he could see Dyrene with no strings attached. Douglas was content with their relationship as long as he dated Dyrene on *his* terms. However, word on the street had a different story. Apparently, Douglas was known to have a few pity parties of his own during their time apart.

***

The Adjustment Bureau came out of retirement and went to work. They had to reset and use their "FOR EMERGENCY USE ONLY" strategy. They created an opportunity for Dyrene to meet this tall, kind, charming, and chocolate brother at a conference. He was a professor at one of the leading universities in Michigan. The brother was single and drop-dead f-i-n-e! We will call him KBL. They exchanged numbers and went their separate ways.

He called Dyrene several times, but deep down, she really was not ready to date. She would blow him off, but finally, Dyrene *did* go out with KBL. He tried to win Dyrene's heart with beautiful flowers, romantic dinners, and other special outings. He was definitely dating *her*, but she was not dating *him*. She could not get over Douglas.

Dyrene found herself talking about Douglas while on dates with KBL. Even with his good looks, charm, and status, KBL still could not break through to touch her heart. After noticing how Dyrene would make herself available for Douglas whenever he called, KBL finally realized he did not have a ghost of a chance.

In reality, the brother never had a chance!

He was unaware he was just a pawn in The Adjustment Bureau's scheme to reunite Douglas and Dyrene.

Instead of continuing to pursue Dyrene, KBL gave her some valuable instructions; advice that would prove fruitful. I guess you can say he was the original author of the think like a man concept. KBL told Dyrene that she had to stop being readily available if she *really* wanted Douglas back. He offered her suggestions to be at home, but *not* be at home. "When Douglas comes calling," he suggested. "Don't answer the door or the phone, even if you are home. Also, visit your sister and friends, but by all means, do *not* be available for Douglas if you want to get him back and to the altar."

That worked! When Dyrene cleared her

head, she also recollected one of her mother's many wise sayings regarding men. Her mother would say, "Why buy the cow when you can get the milk free?" She heeded the advice of KBL and her mother's wise saying. Then, Dyrene did her own disappearing act.

Chapter 10:

The Harvest: Completion! The Wedding

After Douglas could no longer see Dyrene when he wanted to, he came back very strong! Douglas started singing Maze's "Before I Let Go" before he got on one knee and proposed to Dyrene. He said he could not live without her and would rather take a chance on marriage than lose her. She made him sweat for a while before she said yes! He wanted to set a wedding date as soon as possible. It was the month of May 1990 when Douglas proposed. He suggested a fall wedding since they first met in September.

Dyrene found that romantic, so she agreed. Douglas also actively participated in the planning of their wedding. They attended separate pre-marriage counseling sessions with Douglas's brother, the late Rev. Johnnie Saulsberry, and with a non-relative, Rev. Kearney. Douglas and Dyrene were given an assignment during one of their counseling sessions. They were instructed to fold a sheet of paper in half and list each other's strengths and weaknesses. If the items on the weakness side outnumbered the strengths, walk away.

Dyrene listed only one item or challenge she had with Douglas. It was his procrastination/tardiness, but she said she could live with that. His tardiness was not a deal-breaker, citing Douglas was tardy the first day they met at the volunteer program. Also, the pastor offered her some good advice on how to deal with that item, and it still works after 31 years of marriage.

Apparently, the list Douglas created also passed the test. Together, they planned their wedding and waited in anticipation for the day they would say their vows. They had only four months to make the arrangements, but that was not a problem since Dyrene is the ultimate event planner/coordinator. The engagement brunch, wedding rehearsal and rehearsal dinner, a spectacular wedding and reception, a post-wedding day family brunch, and honeymoon were planned and executed without a glitch.

They chose their guiding scripture:

"Delight thyself in the Lord and He will give you the desires of your heart."

Psalm 37:4

Douglas arranged for the nationally renowned harpist Sylvia Holyfield to play "The Wedding Song" for Dyrene's grand entrance. He hired the best limousine service in the Detroit area to transport Dyrene, her mother, and the bridal party to the church. Douglas arrived at the church (on time), but there was no Dyrene. He was baffled and became agitated because he knew she was always punctual. Douglas wondered if the limo driver had gotten lost. Cell phones were not popular back then. Therefore, he could not contact the driver.

In the holding area of the church, three of Douglas's groomsmen—Oscar, Reggie, and Daniel—watched as he paced back and forth. It was unseasonably hot for September. The church had no air conditioning, and sweat poured down Douglas's face like drops of blood. He was a nervous wreck!

Meanwhile, Dyrene, her mother, and the bridal party—Arnita, Evangeline, and Carrie—were at Dyrene's duplex enjoying a beautiful wedding day brunch prepared by her maid of honor. Dyrene's mother noticed the limousine parked out front. She suggested they leave for the church so they would not be late. Dyrene purposely stalled because, based on Douglas's track record, she *knew* he would not be on time; *she* did not want to be the one waiting for *him*.

On September 22, 1990, Dyrene walked down the aisle of Greater Southern Missionary Baptist Church at 1:20 p.m. Her brother Tommy Penn escorted her, and she and Douglas were joined in holy matrimony, becoming husband and wife for life.

The Vows they shared on September 22, 1990, were as follows:

Dyrene

Today is a dream come true for me. I feel so blessed to be marrying my best friend. You have always been my friend. You have always seen in me what no other could see. (I love you for that.)

Before God, our family, and friends, I want you to know that I love and respect you very much. I will always be there for you. That comes easy for me because you continuously show me how much you love and respect me. I know ours is a mutual love affair, and I feel honored to be your wife. I thank God for me, for you, and for us, and for giving us the desires of our hearts.

Douglas

Dyrene Penn, in about 5 seconds, soon-to- be Mrs. Saulsberry, I love you very much! You are my best friend, my best pal, best buddy, best woman, and my best Christian woman. I also thank God for bringing us together. I think God sent us to be together.

I am looking forward to spending the rest of my natural life with you. I could not begin to live life without you. I will always be here for you. I love you very much.

A grand afternoon reception was held at Marygrove College Alumni Hall. The following day, they continued their celebration with a marvelous brunch for family and friends at the fabulous historic Hotel St. Regis.

The next day, Douglas and Dyrene traveled to their honeymoon destination, the famous Poconos Mountains Resort. Their two-story honeymoon suite was beautifully decorated and equipped with a heart-shaped swimming pool and a bathtub in the shape of a champagne glass. With that said, need I say more?

AFTER THE HONEYMOON

O n their first anniversary, Douglas revealed that he regretted wasting so much time, and he wished that he had not been so reluctant to take the next step in their relationship and proposed sooner. He said he enjoyed being married and was looking forward to spending many more years together as husband and wife.

Douglas and Dyrene's wedding was not the end of their story. They have been in total wedded bliss for 31+ years. They renewed their vows in 1999 in an elaborate African-inspired ceremony in Detroit, where they jumped the broom. In 2017, they recommitted their vows at the enchanting Villa Bennmaya Resort in Ocho Rios, Jamaica. Today, they pledge to continue to love and cherish each other for better, for worse, for richer, for poorer, in sickness and in health, until parted by death.

Their Journey Continues...

Epilogue

The subjects of this amazing love story were asked to tell why they love each other in their own words.

WHY DOES DOUGLAS LOVE DYRENE OULEY?

Was it love at first sight? No, it was not even love at second sight. It was more curiosity than anything else. Who was this lady in the swimsuit at the downtown Detroit YMCA volunteering in a program for autistic children? Was it for college credit? Was it because she had a free Saturday morning? Was she genuinely interested in learning about autism? Or was it because she was a good person and she genuinely wanted to make a difference in a young person's life?

After being married to this attractive, talented, and intelligent woman for 31 years, I can honestly say it was all of the above. But the one thing that has stood out over all these years is that she is a good person. She is dependable, ethical, honest, respectable, considerate, loyal, reliable, and moral, and her character is above reproach.

I have always been attracted to a woman's brains more than her body or looks. What is inside the head has always been a tremendous turn-on for me. Dyrene has fit that bill from day one and continues to this day to astound me with her intellect.

We were friends for years, but things began to change one day, and we became *best* friends. I began to see her in a new light. It was like someone said, "Douglas, what you are looking for is right here in front of your eyes."

We shared and agreed in the same belief system and core values. Dyrene had ambition. She was responsible. She was selfless. She fits right in with my family and friends. I have already mentioned being attractive and intelligent. But, most of all, I knew that she loved me unconditionally with all my flaws, and I do have many.

She has brought so much love, joy, and excitement to my life. She turns me on and has definitely made me a better man and brought out the best in me. How could I *not* love and be in love with a person who has *those* qualities? Brains, beauty, and booty!! Man, I hit the jackpot!!! Dyrene Ouley Penn Saulsberry is truly my African Queen. God has given me a blessing more incredible than anything I could ever imagine. I love her with all my heart and soul, and I thank her for being my wife (bride) of 31 years.

Why does Dyrene Ouley Love Douglas?

L et me tell you about my Douglas. Douglas and I did not think of each other as possible lovers when we met. We saw each other as two individuals providing a valuable service to our community. I was seeing someone, and if I were not already in a relationship, I probably would not have been attracted to Douglas.

Initially, I thought he was a little weird. He used bottled water before it became popular. He made carrot juice, and his hands were orange from drinking so much of it. He did not eat pork or beef or smoke cigarettes like I did. In fact, he had a sign on his door that read "No Smoking," so I *knew* we would not get anywhere. You get the picture. It seemed as though we had nothing in common, but I knew he was a nice guy. Always the perfect gentleman! He still opens doors for me and makes sure I am okay.

After getting to know Douglas, I realized I had not met a man like him before. He is God-fearing, handsome, intelligent, health-conscious, sharp dresser, cool, caring, honest, has a good work ethic, trustworthy, dependable, knows his way around the kitchen, and can clean too? I could go on and on about this man. I love his temperament; he is the eternal optimist in *every* situation. When things look dreary, he always sees the positive side. We share common values and morals. Most of all, he has a relationship with Christ.

Another thing that impressed me was the way Douglas treated his mother. After his father passed, Douglas gave up his bachelor's pad and moved into his mother's house to help take care of her. That spoke volumes to me! They said you can always tell how a man will treat you by the way he treats his mother. He was good to his mother, and he treats me like a queen. Douglas also dotes on his cousins, nieces, and nephews. He loves his family!

Douglas has always supported me through my highs and lows. He never judged me, and he accepted me and all my flaws. My love for Douglas grew out of the beautiful friendship we created, shared, and have maintained over the years. He is a positive, motivating force in my life. I often say that I went down a few alleys before getting to Douglas, the avenue.

After all these years, he *still* turns me on. I feel the same sensation I felt when we first fell in love—all giddy, like a young girl. I wake up every day with peace and joy in my heart, thanking God for this incredible man of God who respects and treasures me. Douglas gave me a reason to love again!

I look forward to 31 more years of wedded bliss. We are definitely best friends who happen to be married.

When Douglas Met Dyrene

THE ADJUSTMENT BUREAU'S WORDS:

God created Douglas and Dyrene for each other. We had to make many adjustments to ensure they would find each other, develop a friendship/relationship, and get married. That was the plan! They overcame many obstacles, but we got them to the altar! Mission finally accomplished!

When Douglas Met Dyrene

Appendix

The following are a collection of letters, thoughts, and notes from the couples extraordinary life together.

The Last Vitamin

Douglas and I enjoy eating daily meals together. However, our weekday schedule doesn't allow us to eat breakfast together during the school year. Douglas has to leave for work before I do, so he's the first to eat breakfast.

After I had finished my breakfast, I reached for one of our vitamin bottles and noticed there was only one vitamin left. I didn't take the last vitamin, saving it for the next day for Douglas. The next morning, I noticed that the same vitamin bottle was on the table with one last vitamin. I was baffled! Douglas had already eaten breakfast and left for work. I just knew he had taken the last vitamin and discarded the bottle. The same thing happened the next day! Why? What is happening here, I wondered? Why does this bottle keep appearing? During dinner, we discussed the mystery of the last vitamin. Douglas said, "Sweetheart, I was saving it for you," and of course, I said, "Honey, I was saving it for you." We had a great laugh and a FANTASTIC EVENING!!!

LETTER TO DOUGLAS FROM DYRENE: 2/20/1985

Dearest Douglas,

By now, you are probably sick of me, but who cares (smile). What are friends for? Seriously though, I do appreciate your being patient with me. You do not know how much it helps me to hear your voice when I am distraught. (Boy, I love you so much. I often wish you were mine.)

You told me recently that you are confused about the lady you were seeing; well, I have always been confused about you. Most of the time, my love for you is stronger than one of a friendship type love. It scares the hell out of me because I know we are supposed to be just friends. One thing I do know is that I love you very much as a friend and that is where all relationships should begin (with friendship); so, if fate has it so that you and I have a future together someday, at least we do honestly love one another. We are friends!

Doug, I hope you can comprehend this letter. I am writing you from my desk at work. Ms. Harms has popped in here twice for some information, so I might seem incoherent…. Talk to you later.

Your friend, Dee

#1 - My Special Friends

"I met my special friends in the late '70's—we were all teachers at Oakman. Even then, Douglas and Dyrene were close---often observed sharing lunch or a private conversation.

In between the parties, luncheons, and fun times, I watched as my friends met the challenges of life: failed relationships/marriage, birth, and even death. Dyrene even tried to "hook me up" with her buddy Douglas because he deserved someone "nice." At the time, I was struggling to make an impossible relationship work and not open to the idea. A few years later, she announced that she found someone for Doug - "I'm keeping him for myself."

October 29, 1985, my friend wrote, "I am in love with him. I never thought I could feel this way about Doug." When I got married to my best friend in 1988, my friend Douglas asked, "How did you know you wanted to get married?" Maybe I said something right…the Saulsberrys were married two years later.

There are many acquaintances along the way with very few true friends…today I honor my Special Friends, Douglas and Ouley, for more than 20 years of unconditional friendship. May God continue to bless you.

Love you both,

Patty

#2 - ANOTHER NOTE FROM A SPECIAL FRIEND- 9/1999

To my dear friends, Doug and Ouley. Through the years that I have known you both, I have become an admirer of your relationship. You have much happiness, and I know it is a happiness of being connected, of trusting completely, and knowing that the one you trust is the one you love. You both have a strong sense of ethnic identity and pride. You are faithful to each other and make sacrifices for each other.

You both have strong spiritual values and share concerns and feelings. These are elements I believe for a very strong and enduring marriage.

Much happiness to you both, and may you always remain soul mates.

Love you both.

Your friend, Kathy

#3 - Excerpt from a letter written by Cousin Nita 4/4/2000

"It is Tuesday, and you have been on my mind since last evening. I came across something as I was cleaning out drawers. It was a program from you and Doug's 9th anniversary celebration. It was "9 Steps to Spice up a Marriage". When I was first given this package of information, I could not appreciate it as much since I had only been married one month. Seven months later, I came to see the real beauty underneath all of what was written."

"Dyrene, what I am saying is that you are one woman that I can say demonstrates what it takes to keep a marriage alive! No, I do not know what *goes on behind closed doors on Balfour Road, but what you do display in public is genuine love, trust and support of your husband and marriage. I personally do not know of any other woman who has your same demeanor about marriage. Never once have I heard any negativity or lack of support for your husband. Never have I heard you speak any unkind word about Douglas or marriage.*

"Being married myself in this short length of time, I have learned it is challenging and calls for "adjustments". However, your approach in marriage appears so smooth, so calm, so loving. Your marriage encourages me to want to just always be in love and having honeymoons over and over." I know it takes two to make a marriage and that an understanding husband helps. However, I am just toasting you this time because I hear too much of

"husband bashing" and "marriage bashing" from women."

Yes, you do have a story to tell and maybe someday you will put it all in writing. Keep up the good work!

TOPICS AND QUESTIONS TO PONDER

1. At the beginning of the story, Dyrene bid her family farewell at a young age and moved to Detroit, Michigan, to pursue her dream of becoming a teacher. What do you think of Dyrene's decision to leave her roots at an early age? Did you ever make a life-changing decision? If so, what was the outcome? What does the move say about Dyrene's overall character?

2. The Adjustment Bureau would not stop

at anything to complete its mission of bringing Douglas and Dyrene together. Do you think they would go as far as cause a tragedy in the singing group to keep Douglas on a certain path? Why or why not?

3. What is your opinion of KBL? Do you think he fought hard enough to win Dyrene's affection?

4. Dyrene let it be known that she wanted more than a "friends with benefits" relationship with Douglas. What do you think about Douglas wanting to have both his cake and ice cream?

5. Douglas's decision to call off their court-ship caused Dyrene great pain. Do you think she should have taken him back after the breakup?

6. Douglas and Dyrene experienced a pla-tonic friendship for almost a decade. Have you or anyone you know main-tained a long-standing male-female re-lationship? What factors do you think contribute to sustaining a long-term friendship?

7. Did you or someone you know cross the line and date and/or marry your best friend? What was the result of

your/their decision? Do you think it is realistic or possible to have a male-female platonic relationship?

8. What evidence in the story suggests that Dyrene followed God's plan for her life?

Words from the Author

I thank God for the opportunity to share Douglas's and my love story. It has been an exciting journey. While writing our story, I fell in love with Douglas repeatedly, with each stroke of the pen. Writing our story was exhilarating! I relived so many precious memories. I cried happy and sad tears, and I also laughed.

Our story is honest and raw, one we were willing to share in hopes of entertaining and enlightening the readers about our personal journey and providing encouragement. Whatever you do, do not give up on love.

Who knows, Mr. Right or Ms. Right could be right in front of your eyes. The Adjustment Bureau is available to all!

ACKNOWLEDGMENTS

Jesus Christ: Executive Producer

Annie Kuykendall: Cover Photo

I also would like to send a heavenly thank you to the woman who gave me life, my mother Mrs. Izora Howard Penn. Lastly, a special thank you to Min. Maxine Stephens and Deborah Hanna for your encouragement, support, and working behind the scenes to help create this amazing love story. I truly appreciate you.

STAY TUNED FOR DYRENE'S NOVEL TITLED:

Our Incredible Path to Love

Made in the USA
Middletown, DE
02 February 2024

48463593R00068